more
curious
JANE

STERLING CHILDREN'S BOOKS
New York

An Imprint of Sterling Publishing Co., Inc.
1166 Avenue of the Americas
New York, NY 10036

ISBN 978-1-4549-3134-8

Distributed in Canada by Sterling Publishing Co., Inc.
c/o Canadian Manda Group, 664 Annette Street
Toronto, Ontario M6S 2C8, Canada
Distributed in the United Kingdom by GMC Distribution Services
Castle Place, 166 High Street, Lewes, East Sussex BN7 1XU, England
Distributed in Australia by NewSouth Books
University of New South Wales, Sydney, NSW 2052, Australia

For information about custom editions, special sales, and premium and corporate purchases, please
contact Sterling Special Sales at 800-805-5489 or specialsales@sterlingpublishing.com.

Manufactured in China

Lot #:
2 4 6 8 10 9 7 5 3 1
10/18

sterlingpublishing.com

Illustrations by Elissa Josse and Bethany Robertson
Photography by Caroline Kaye

www.curiousjanecamp.com

more CURIOUS JANE

science

+

design

+

engineering
for inquisitive girls

STERLING CHILDREN'S BOOKS
New York

Dear Curious Janes,

Welcome to another round of projects from CJ BK, our workspace in Brooklyn!

There are a few different ways you can use this book, and I hope that you do use it a lot! Get goop on the pages, make notes in the margins, mark the projects you want to try first . . . and get started!

One way to use the book is by diving into a specific section that calls to you. Do you like mixing stuff up, experimenting, and getting messy? Go for Kitchen Chemistry. Do you like to make things for other people? Definitely dive into Gifts to Give and Keep. When you pick a specific section, go ahead and gather the supplies you will need to make a bunch of the different projects. And if you don't have something on hand? Improvise and see what happens!

Another way to use the book is by project simplicity or complexity. Do you have a short amount of time, and are you in the mood for something simple? Or do you have a full day to fill and you want to tackle something a little more complex? We've rated each project as easy, medium, or hard to guide you in picking projects.

And of course, you can always use the book by mood. Feeling patient? Go for Geode Eggs or Soapsicles. Feeling active? Try the Stomp Rocket. Feel like getting messy? Definitely go for Moon Sand or Slimy Crafts. You get the idea!

Or just close your eyes, open the book, and start on that page in the middle. Try it!

Two tips:

Collect your supplies and set up your maker station. Take the time to do this at the start, and it will smooth your way for plenty of invention and creativity.

And my favorite all-time maker philosophy: *let your hands do the thinking.*

We're excited and honored that you are trying these projects. We've collected them for you! Now take them and make them Your Own.

Happy Making!

Samantha

contents

i love this stuff

kitchen chemistry

equal parts chemistry, recipe experimentation, and fun!

spherification: eat a drink!

Spherification is the culinary process of shaping liquids into spheres!

Watch sheer little membranes form to hold liquid inside. Hold them in your hands, poke them, and watch them jiggle—then pop one into your mouth! Enjoy a burst of water or juice!

Really awesome

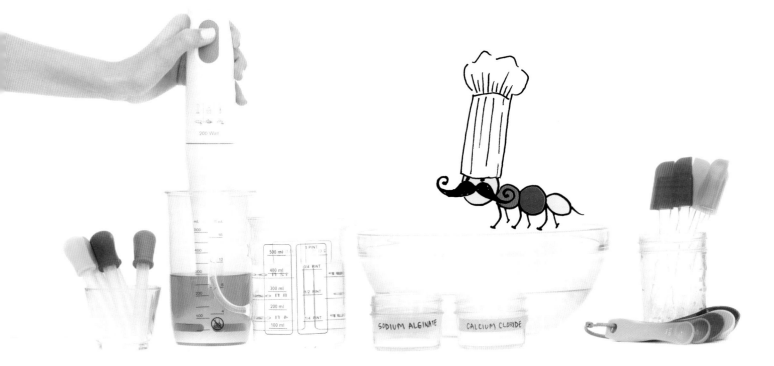

maker checklist

small bowls or cups

2 large bowls

measuring cup

measuring spoons

dropper or pipette

slotted spoon

immersion blender

juice or other drink

sodium alginate
   (seaweed extract!)

water

calcium chloride
   (powdered calcium!)

These unusual ingredients are used in the food industry and can easily be found online!

sodium alginate + juice mixture

What makes this project work is the way in which sodium alginate combines with calcium. The alginate can thicken and bind without heat, and does so when exposed to calcium. Voilà, you've got an edible drink!

calcium chloride + water bath

 In a small bowl, combine 1½ cups of juice with ½ teaspoon of sodium alginate.

 Use the immersion blender to completely dissolve the powder and blend the mixture together. The mixture will look cloudy since it's filled with air bubbles! Let it sit for 15 minutes until it looks clear.

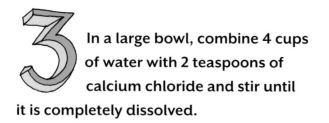 In a large bowl, combine 4 cups of water with 2 teaspoons of calcium chloride and stir until it is completely dissolved.

Use a dropper or pipette to drop your sodium alginate + juice mixture into your calcium chloride + water bath.

 Let your juice-bead spheres set for a few minutes without touching them; the longer they stay in the water bath, the more solid they will get.

 Using a slotted spoon, gently move the spheres from the calcium chloride mixture into the second large bowl filled with clean water; this rinse will stop the reaction.

7 Carefully lift your juice beads out of the water and pop them into your mouth! So weird and so cool!

now we're gonna get fancy on ya!

what's **molecular gastronomy** and why should you care?

Molecular gastronomy is a type of food science that explores the physical and chemical changes that occur in cooking. Its focus is more on the home cook and restaurant cooking than on mass-produced foods. The term *molecular gastronomy* was coined in 1988 by a physicist and a chemist, but studying science that occurs when cooking, called *food science*, is a much older concept.

crazy cool

tools + techniques used to play around with molecular gastronomy

immersion blender,
ice cream maker,
foams and things that fizz, and . . .
spherification!

you just changed a liquid into a semi-solid. and that's not something you get to do every day.

difficulty: easy

bouncy
eggs

maker checklist

1 egg

clean jar with lid

distilled vinegar

Much of this chapter is about things changing form. Dissolving, disappearing, growing, melting, moving from solid to liquid and vice versa. With this cool project, we make an egg shell disappear, revealing what's inside and creating a bouncy oval object.

Place your egg in the jar very carefully. (Laying the jar on its side or using a spoon helps!)

2 Fill the jar with vinegar and screw the lid on tightly.

3 Let sit for about five days and watch the shell disappear!

yes, that's the shell!

what is happening?

Vinegar contains acetic acid. This reacts with the high calcium content of the eggshell and dissolves it!

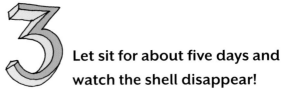

geode eggs

crystallization and sedimentation

This activity combines both of these things! It demonstrates how geodes are formed in real life, and the result can be beautiful. Use Epsom salts or alum powder as a "growing agent" for your egg crystals. Be patient and have fun!

what is a GEODE?

a small cavity in rock lined with crystals and other mineral matter.

what is sedimentation?

the process by which particles (solute) suspended in fluid (solvent) eventually come to rest due to the forces, such as gravity, that act upon them.

what is crystallization?

this process forms crystals or crystalline structures (snowflakes are an example).

what is a super-saturated solution?

when the water in your solution has absorbed all it is able to absorb and any other solid you add will not dissolve.

maker checklist

plenty of eggs

2 bowls

egg carton or mini-muffin tin

saucepan + spoon

measuring cups + water

food coloring in bright colors

toothpicks

school glue + brush (optional)

AND any soluble solid:

Epsom salt (our favorite)

table, rock, or kosher salt

granulated sugar

baking soda

cream of tartar

alum powder

this will form your geode!

1 Crack the egg at the narrow end (just a tiny crack!) and carefully open it over a bowl. Save the inside of the egg for cooking or baking! Here we're just working with the shell—your goal is to have one or two eggshell halves that are large enough to hold liquid.

2 Set the shells in a bowl of hot water to rinse them off and soften the membrane.

3 Gently rub your thumb against the inside of the shell to loosen the membrane and peel it out of the shell. (There may be two layers—make sure to remove all of it!)

4 *Optional step*: Brush the inside of your dry shells with a thin layer of school glue; dust with a layer of soluble solid. This will act as a starter crystal. Let dry completely.

5 Turn the shells over on a paper towel to dry, then set them in the egg carton (or mini-muffin tin) so that they are stable and you can pour liquid into them.

6 Boil 1 cup of water (use the stove or microwave) and carefully remove from the heat.

7 Add ½ cup Epsom salt (or any soluble solid) and stir until it is dissolved.

8 Continue stirring in small amounts of the solid (a tablespoon or two at a time) until it no longer dissolves, then stop! This means the water has absorbed all the solid it can and your solution is super-saturated.

9 Carefully pour the solution into your prepared shells, right to the top.

10 Add a drop of food coloring to each egg and gently stir with a toothpick.

11 Place your shells where they will be undisturbed for at least a few days.

12 Crystals will form inside the eggshells as the water evaporates.

tend to your geodes!

You may need to tend to your geodes! Check your geodes daily. If you find that a thin, hard layer is forming on the surface, gently break this up with a toothpick. Opening the solution up will allow the water to continue to evaporate.

s'mores pizza

maker checklist

ruler + pencil

1 small pizza box

scissors or craft knife
(with adult help)

2 sheets aluminum foil

masking tape

1 sheet black paper

1 piece transparency film
(from office supply store)

skewer or thin dowel

and . . . your s'more!

2 graham crackers

1 marshmallow

1 chocolate square

 Measure and mark a square on the top of your box, about 1 inch from each edge. Cut three sides to make a flap.

 Line the inside of the flap and the bottom of the box with foil, taping the edges to keep it in place.

 Cut a square of black paper larger than the s'more you want to make and tape this onto the foil in the center of the bottom of the box.

 Cover the opening in the box top with the transparency film. Tape into place on the inside, so that the entire opening is covered, like a window.

box solar oven

Place a s'more on the black paper, close the lid, and prop open the flap using the skewer.

Set in a sunny spot and bake! Position it so the sun bounces off the foil and into the oven. The heat is trapped inside, so your s'more will bake!

powered by the sun!

Solar S'MORES oven

basic slime recipe

use this recipe as the starting point for all of your slime experiments

did you know?

slime is a non-Newtonian fluid

Non-Newtonian fluids are ones that misbehave. They will change if you heat, squeeze, stir, or press on them. They can feel more like liquids or more like solids, depending on how much force you apply to them.

A·maz·ing

 Measure ¼ cup of school glue (white or clear, depending on the project) into a cup.

 Add food coloring into the glue—drop by drop—and stir well for a consistent color.

 Mix glitter, if using, and 1 tablespoon liquid starch into the glue. Stir quickly and carefully to combine.

 Knead the resulting goopy stuff until it becomes even in consistency.

maker checklist

measuring cups + spoons

clear or white school glue

plastic cups + stir sticks

food coloring +
    glitter (optional)

liquid starch

you've got slime!

quick ratios for slime

glue	¼ cup	½ cup	1 cup
starch	1 tbsp	2 tbsp	¼ cup

each recipe uses either white or clear school glue.

Liquid Starch

SCHOOL GLUE

sparkly sun catchers

make: basic slime recipe with clear glue

maker checklist

basic slime (from the basic slime recipe on page 22)

small plastic plates, plastic containers, or petri dishes

glitter (for sparkle, optional)

YAY!

Make your basic slime using clear glue. Next, mix small batches of translucent slime in a variety of beautiful colors. Add glitter if you want your slime to sparkle. If the slime is too sticky, use less starch, or let it sit for a while to thicken up.

 Press small bits of slime into a small plastic plate, shallow plastic container, or petri dish.

 Let it sit uncovered for a few hours or overnight. The slime will settle into a smooth, shiny layer.

Peel the slime out of the dish and press against a sunny window. It will slowly drip down the window, changing shape as it goes!

difficulty: *easy*

super-sticky slimy putty

make: basic slime recipe with white glue

1 Make your basic slime using white glue. Next, mix small batches of opaque slime in a palette of colors.

2 Knead thoroughly until it does not stick to your hands.

3 Let it sit out for a few hours or overnight. It will thicken into putty.

slimy putty magic word transfer

Using a black marker, write a word backward on a piece of paper. Press your slimy putty to it, then peel it away!

shake it, make it butter

the key to making butter? agitation! that's the shaking, so shake things up!

Butter is a fat that has been removed from the milk or cream produced by a cow. Heavy cream is used for making butter, because it contains more butter fat.

SHAKE SHAKE SHAKE

WITH a GREAT DEAL OF BUTTER ON TOP!

1 Fill your jar halfway with heavy cream, add a marble if you have one, and close the jar tightly!

2 Shake it! (Shake it a lot!) This will take about 10 minutes.

when you shake a jar of cream, the cream goes through stages:

First, it becomes whipped cream—whipped with so many air bubbles that the fat globules stick together and form tiny protective coverings over the air pockets.

Then, when the cream doesn't have enough air to whip properly, it clumps into a more solid, spreadable form—butter! The liquid that's left over? Yep, it's buttermilk!

it's butter 3 ways!

Your butter will be delicious on its own, but you can also flavor it if you like.
Try adding:

cinnamon + sugar
chives
smoky paprika

butter

buttermilk

shake-it-yourself ice cream

go ahead and build up your shaking muscles!

★ ☆ ★

important! seal it tight.

make your own

 Fill your large plastic bag about half-full with ice. Add the salt and shake it up until the ice is evenly coated. Then set aside.

 Combine half-and-half, sugar, extract, and a pinch of salt in the small bag. Then seal it tight. Make sure there are no gaps!

 Nestle the small bag of ice cream mixture into the large bag of ice so that the ice surrounds it, then seal the large bag tightly.

4 Shake, shake, shake it up! After about 5 minutes of shaking, it will be ready to eat!

maker checklist

gallon-size sealable plastic bag

4–6 cups of ice

6 tablespoons kosher or rock salt (plus an extra pinch)

½ cup half-and-half

1 tablespoon sugar

½ teaspoon vanilla extract
. . . or any other fruits and flavors!

pint-size sealable plastic bag

how does it happen?

The only way to freeze ice cream is to make sure the stuff around it (in the big bag) is actually colder than the ice that forms inside it (in the little bag). Salt slightly changes the boiling and freezing temperatures for water. When you add salt to the ice cubes, it causes them to melt faster (like when you throw salt on an icy sidewalk), but the resulting salt water is actually *colder* than regular ice. Eventually that water will warm up, but as long as there are still a few ice cubes in the bag, you know that the surrounding salt water is colder than ice.

gifts to give + keep

when you create a gift for someone, you are also sharing your ideas, energy, and personality.

difficulty: medium
soapsicles!

1 Melt the desired amount of glycerin (enough for your first layer) in a microwave-safe measuring cup.

tip: **start by heating for 30 seconds and continuing in 10-second intervals until liquid.**

maker checklist

white glycerin soap base

microwave-safe measuring cup

soap colorants

funnel

classic ice pop mold

rubbing alcohol in a spray bottle

wooden ice pop sticks

bowl of hot water

we started with white soap base to create bold, opaque colors.

some brands even come in fruity scents!

2 Color the melted glycerin with a few drops of soap colorant. Don't be afraid to mix colors!

you can find a classic ice pop mold online.

these look sweet BUT PLEASE... *don't eat!*

YAY!

soap colorants are easy to find in fun color sets.

a spritz of rubbing alcohol helps reduce the air bubbles between layers.

RASPBERRY
Weight of goods: 0,3 d
Dosage: 1-5 drops
3 ounces of soap.
Shake before use!

BRIGHT PINK
Weight of goods: 0,3 d
Dosage: 1-5 drops
3 ounces of soap.
Shake before use!

BRIGHT GREEN
Weight of goods: 0,3 d
Dosage: 1-5 drops
3 ounces of soap.
Shake before use!

PURPLE
Weight of goods: 0,3
Dosage: 1-5 drops
per 3 ounces of soap.
Shake before use!

YELLOW
Weight of goods: 0,3
Dosage: 1-5 drops
per 3 ounces of
Shake before use!

BRIGHT B
Weight of goods: 0,
Dosage: 1-5 drops
per 3 ounces of soap
Shake before use!

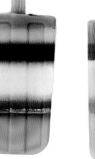

3 Use a funnel to pour the first layer of soap into your ice pop mold.

4 Spray rubbing alcohol onto the poured glycerin to avoid air bubbles. Let harden for 20 minutes.

the funnel prevents soap from splashing up on the inside of the mold. this keeps the layers nice and neat.

rubbing alcohol between layers helps prevent air bubbles.

when you have filled the mold about halfway, put the lid on and insert an ice pop stick—the lid will keep it straight.

 Repeat steps 1–4 to create your next color layer.

tip: This layer should be thick to hold your ice pop stick in place.

 Now, with the mold half full, place the cover on top and insert a wooden ice pop stick. Let sit for 20 minutes.

 Continue with additional layers of color until the mold is full. Refrigerate for several hours.

 Remove the finished soapsicle from the mold by dipping the mold into a bowl of hot water to soften the edges (about one minute). Squeeze the mold gently and "pop" your soapsicle out!

make your own!

colorblock napkins

Plain cotton napkins are inexpensive and absorb the paint well.

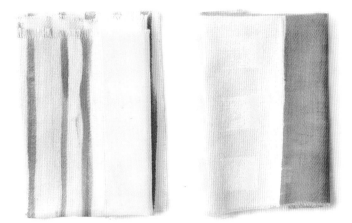

HOW TO
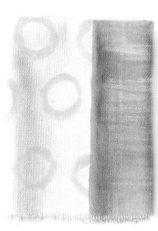

1 Cover your work surface with paper and lay out your napkin so it's nice and flat.

2 Tape the napkin down across the middle with a strip of masking tape.

maker checklist

paper or plastic table cover

masking tape

plain cotton napkins

textile paints

foam brush

we trimmed off the napkin's hem. this leaves a raw edge that beautifully matches the imperfect style of the patterns.

Paint one side a solid color, brushing the color all the way to the edges.

 Accent the other half of the napkin with a fun pattern. Use black or a contrasting color.

 tip: The edges of a foam brush make simple patterns easy!

5 Let dry completely and then enjoy! They can be washed by hand and laid flat to dry, or wiped clean with a cloth.

which is your fave ?

twisty pretzel pillow

1 Cut the waistband off a pair of tights. If you are using footless tights, turn your tights inside out and stitch the feet closed. Then turn them back so that the correct side is facing out.

2 Pull the legs of the tights apart to make one long straight tube.

3 Stuff the tights with polyfill through the opening. Be careful not to overstuff!

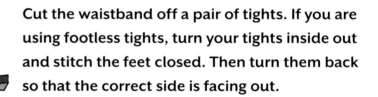

 **4** Stitch the opening closed using a needle and thread.

tip: Fold your cut edges over into the opening before you sew to make a neat, finished edge.

 5 Twist into a pretzel shape and tack down the connection points with a simple stitch so it can keep its shape!

light-up cards

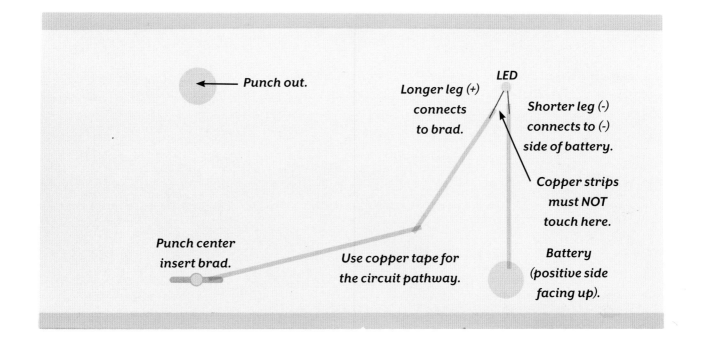

Punch out.

LED

Longer leg (+) connects to brad.

Shorter leg (-) connects to (-) side of battery.

Copper strips must NOT touch here.

Punch center insert brad.

Use copper tape for the circuit pathway.

Battery (positive side facing up).

tip: The key to this circuit is that the brass fastener connects with the coin battery when the card is folded and closed.

1 Plan your circuit! Use our template or create one of your own.

2 Identify the anode (+) and cathode (-) legs of the LED. The anode leg will be longer and have a smaller flag at the top. The cathode leg will be shorter and have a larger flag at the top. The anode leg *must* connect to the positive side of the battery and the cathode leg *must* connect to the negative side of the battery.

maker checklist

LED

white or colored cardstock

¼-inch copper tape

3V coin battery (CR2032)

masking tape

regular hole punch

brass fastener (also called a brad)

colored paper + markers + other craft supplies for decoration

Place your LED onto your card (as shown) so that the cathode leg is on the right. Use a small strip of copper tape to tape the cathode down to the paper and then down to the spot where the battery will be placed. (Separate the legs a bit to make it easier to tape down.)

 Place the negative side of the battery down firmly against the other end of the copper tape. Use masking tape to tape this in place *around the edges* of the battery. (Leave the center exposed! Your fastener will need to connect here.)

 Punch a hole on the left-hand side of the card, insert the fastener from the front, and secure into place.

Using copper tape strips, tape the anode leg down and connect this to the fastener.

tip: Make sure that the two copper tape paths do *not* touch at any point (especially where they connect to the legs of the LED)—this will cause your circuit to short!

Punch out

Longer leg (+) connects to brad.

Shorter leg (-) connects to (-) side of battery.

Copper strips must not touch here.

Punch center and insert brad.

Use copper tape for the circuit pathway.

Battery positive side facing up.

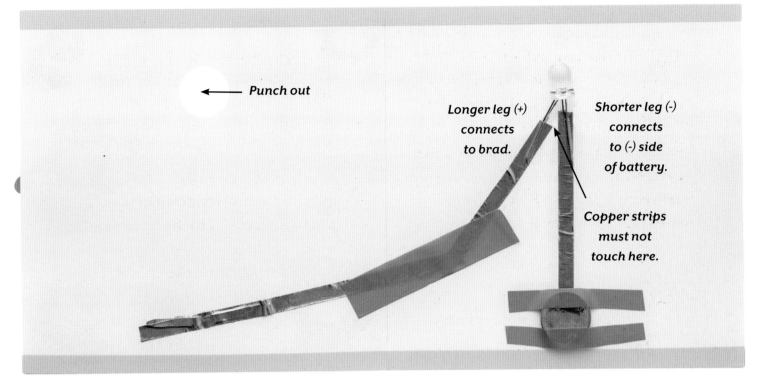

← *Punch out*

Longer leg (+) connects to brad.

Shorter leg (-) connects to (-) side of battery.

Copper strips must not touch here.

 **7** Punch or cut a larger hole on the left-hand side of the card to expose the LED when the card is folded in half.

 **8** Now, close the card, pressing the fastener against the battery, and your LED will light up!

 **9** Once your circuit is set, decorate the front of your card!

troubleshoot tips!

If your LED is not lighting up, you can troubleshoot! Make sure the battery and LED are working by testing them directly. Squeeze the anode leg against the positive side and the cathode against the negative side. (It won't shock you!) Replace the battery or LED as needed.

Make sure that your copper tape is firmly in place, making a strong connection. Also make sure that the paths do not touch one another. Once the circuit is working, you can cover the copper tape paths with masking tape to ensure that they don't cross when the card is folded and closed.

super simple
scratch-off
cards

i love this stuff

maker checklist

paper + markers

card stock

clear packing tape

masking tape

acrylic paint + brush

liquid dish soap

1 Design your card with a secret scratch-off message, and cover this section with clear packing tape.

2 Mask with masking tape for a clean edge.

tip: Try the tape on a scrap piece of paper first to make sure it won't tear the paper.

3 Create the scratch-off mixture by combining 2 parts acrylic paint with 1 part dish soap—stir gently so you don't create too many bubbles!

4 Paint over your secret message and let dry completely.

5 Peel off the masking tape and voilà! Your very own scratch-off card.

scratch with a coin to reveal the secret message

you have permission to space out!

stomp rocket

crazy cool

give it a stomp and see it fly!

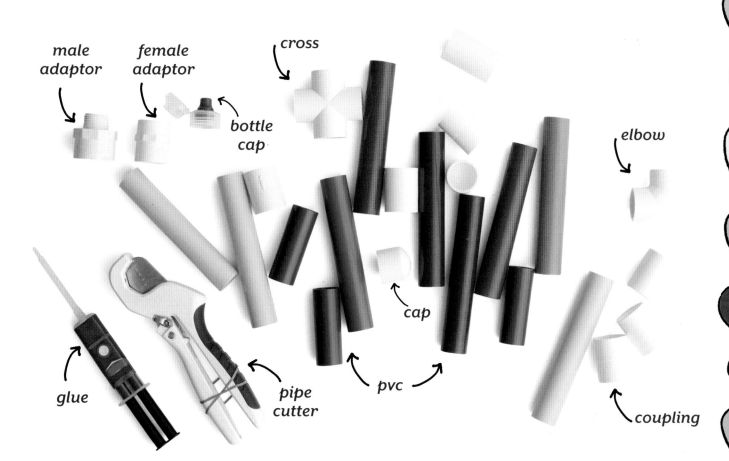

male adaptor

female adaptor

cross

bottle cap

elbow

glue

pipe cutter

cap

pvc

coupling

maker checklist

6 feet of ¾-inch PVC pipe (white or color)

and the following PVC fittings:

1 cross

7 couplings

1 elbow

2 caps

1 male adapter

1 female adapter

PVC pipe cutter

plastic-to-plastic
  adhesive

sports bottle cap

rubber band

for the rocket:

paper, pencil, scissors

masking tape + double-stick tape

glue

for the stomp:

2-liter plastic bottle, empty!

Wrap a rubber band around the base.

HOW TO
build the launch pad:

1

Cut the PVC into nine 6-inch sections and three 3-inch sections. Set aside.

2

Using plastic-to-plastic adhesive, glue the sports bottle cap into the male adapter. To get a secure connection, wrap a rubber band around the base of the cap a few times. Insert it into the connector, and fill the seam with glue.

3

Attach the male adapter to the female adapter and then to the first piece of 6-inch PVC, like you see in the photo below.

tinker more!

air tube

↙ *male adaptor*   *PVC* ↘

↖ *female adaptor*

stabilizing crossbar

air tube

this section attaches vertically and the rocket is placed at the top.

4

Lay out your components, and assemble them as shown in the photo above. The piece with the male adapter will be at one end, connecting to a long air tube with a stabilizing crossbar.

build the rocket:

building a snug-fitting rocket is surprisingly tricky, even though it's just paper! here we show you the tricks . . .

 1 Wrap a piece of 8½ × 11–inch paper snugly around the remaining length of PVC. Tape it in place. This adds a bit of thickness to the PVC so that when you construct the paper rocket, it slides perfectly onto the PVC—not too tight, not too loose.

2 Wrap another piece of sturdy colorful paper around the bulked-up PVC. Tape this paper to itself, but not to the PVC. Tape along the seam and slide it off. Now you have a perfect paper tube!

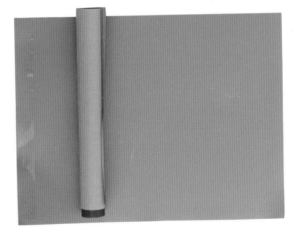

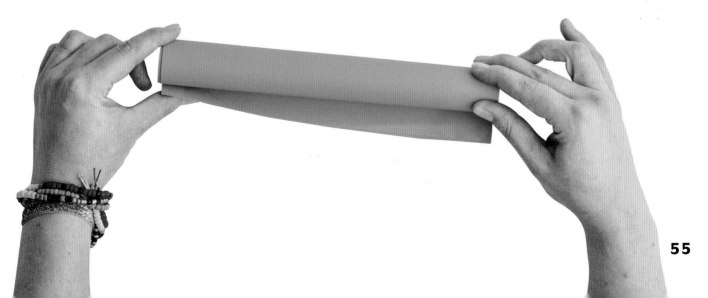

Cut and construct 3 fins and a nose cone. (See the shapes to the right to determine what you will need.) Securely glue or tape into place on your rocket. Now, using the paper-wrapped PVC as your base and the templates for fins and nose cones, make as many rockets as you like!

nose cone

fins

the nose cone is the tricky part!

make sure the tip of the nose cone is closed so that air can't get through. use a spot of tape to seal it if you need to.

make your own!

you might need a lot of rockets!

use a 3-inch piece of PVC at the top of the rocket launcher. the rocket will slide perfectly and rest on the coupling.

ready to
stomp!

place your rocket on the vertical top of the rocket launcher, and screw the 2-liter bottle in securely at the other end. rev up, stomp, and launch!

THE SCIENCE BEHIND IT

when you smash the air in the bottle into the small space of the tube, you are creating a high-pressure area, and it has to come out somewhere! the pressure races up into the paper rocket (which is resting at normal air pressure) and launches it off the PVC pipe. air naturally wants to move from high pressure to low pressure, even if that means going up, like a rocket. that's force!

What do you call an alien with three eyes?

An aliiien!

it's messy to make but easy to clean. it's part soap, after all!

difficulty: *easy*

moon sand

maker checklist

- big bag of baking soda
- a couple tins of baking powder
- measuring cups
- mixing bowl + spoon
- liquid dish soap
- food coloring (optional)

once in a blue moon

to do something "once in a blue moon" means to do it very rarely. the phrase refers to the appearance of a second full moon within a calendar month, and this happens only about every thirty-two months.

1 Combine 2 parts baking soda and 1 part baking powder in a large mixing bowl. We used 2 cups of baking soda and 1 cup of baking powder, but use whatever measurement you want, as long as you're consistent in ratio!

2 Now add 1 part (for us, 1 cup) of dish soap and stir well. You can start with a spoon, but as it combines, it's more fun to use your hands.

 **3** Color with food coloring (optional) and play!

it won't store long. enjoy it for a day, then throw it away!

glow-in-the-dark gelatin

make your gelatin with tonic water, instead of tap water, and it will glow under a black light!

crazy cool

what is happening here?

A substance called quinine makes tonic water glow under a black light. *Quinine* comes from a kind of tree bark; it's what gives tonic its bitter taste and blue glow. Long ago, quinine was used to treat a sickness called malaria. It no longer is, but small amounts of it are used in tonic water, and it's the secret ingredient that makes this gelatin glow.

but how?

Quinine is *fluorescent*. This means it gives off light of one color whenever it is exposed to light of another color from another source. We exposed quinine to *ultraviolet light*—this is the invisible component of sunlight that produces suntans and sunburns. The structure of the quinine molecule allows it to take in energy in the form of invisible UV light and instantly radiate some of the same energy in the form of visible blue light.

blacklight DIY!

maker checklist

flashlight (or phone light)

clear tape

royal-blue marker

royal-purple marker

1 Cover your entire light source with clear tape.

2 Color the tape with blue marker, let dry for a half hour, then color again.

3 Apply a second piece of clear tape, and color with purple marker. Voilà!

4 Shine it on something white to test it out. It should glow! Next, shine it on your glow-in-the-dark gelatin!

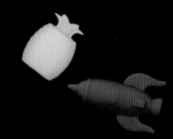

here's how to make
your own blacklight
to make your
projects glow!

cool!

difficulty: *medium*

papier-mâché planets

you can make an out-of-this-world project with a few simple supplies that you probably already have!

 Cover your work surface with newspaper or a plastic tablecloth.

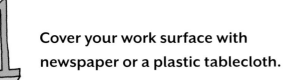 Cut your newspaper into strips about 1 inch wide. You'll want various lengths and you don't need to be exact!

maker checklist

newspaper or plastic tablecloth

scissors

flour + water

large bowl

balloons

paint + brushes

jars or cups (helpful!)

 Create your papier-mâché "glue" by combining 1 part flour with 2 parts water in a large bowl. Mix well until all the lumps are gone. Your mixture should be runny like school glue, not thick like paste. Add more water or flour to get the right consistency.

Blow up your balloon, but don't overinflate! It should be a nice spherical shape that is perfect for a planet.

 tip: Place your balloon on a jar to keep it from rolling around while you work.

 Dip a strip of newspaper into the glue mixture until it's nice and saturated. Gently pinch your fingers along the paper as you remove it to squeeze off the excess glue.

 Cover your balloon with a layer of paper strips, making sure to overlap as you go. Leave the tied end of the balloon uncovered so you can pull it out of the papier-mâché sphere later.

Bonjour Balloon

in french, papier-mâché means "chewed paper"

Super Sweet

7 Let dry and repeat the process a few times. The more times you cover your balloon, the thicker and stronger your planet will be. We found that three layers worked really well!

this one is venus!

as early as 1540, papier-mâché was used to make doll heads!

8 Once your paper strips are all completely dry, paint your papier-mâché planet. Look at pictures of the planets in our solar system for inspiration, or create your very own celestial body! Set it on a jar to dry.

9 Once your paint is dry, pop the balloon and gently wiggle it out from the hole. You can display your planets on a stand. We used dowels and sturdy plastic straws . . . they spin!

difficulty: *hard*

light-up
twirlycopter

these spinning
fliers are super
fun—the light-up
circuit will
brighten
up your twirl!

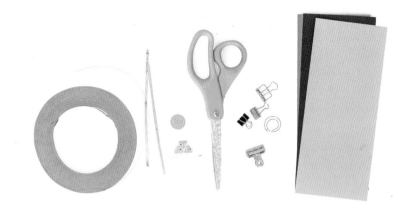

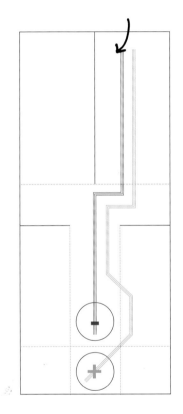

refer to our mini template here (and full size on the next page) when following the steps. and remember: cut along the solid lines; fold along the dotted lines.

1 Cut your paper into a rectangle, 4 × 9½ inches. Make one 4-inch cut down the center from the top (for the two rotors). Make two 1¼-inch cuts on either side, 1 inch below the end of the top slit (to fold in to create the base).

2 Fold the two rotors down on either side of the top slit, and fold the two sides of the base inward. Then fold the bottom portion of the base upward to create a pocket for your battery (about 1 inch).

3 Trace the two circles for the battery on the bottom of the base—one on each side of your bottom fold. Mark them positive and negative.

4 Run one piece of copper tape from the negative battery terminal onto one wing.

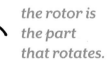

the rotor is the part that rotates.

69

5 Place the second piece of copper tape from the positive battery terminal onto the same wing. Make sure the two pieces of tape are parallel on the wing and will not touch on the base when the bottom is folded up!

6 Connect LED stickers to the copper tape, making sure to attach the positive end of the LED sticker to the positive strip of tape, and the negative to the negative.

7 Add the battery to the base of your copter. Fold the bottom up over the battery and make sure it lights up before you clip it in place.

the science behind it

8 Hold your twirlycopter from the base with your arm held high (or stand a few steps up on a staircase) and drop it to watch it twirl!

troubleshoot tips!

copper tape can be a bit finicky. make sure you overlap the tape at corners and press down firmly to make strong connections. remember that LED stickers (like LED lights) have polarity—an anode (+) and a cathode (-) side. the anode must have a direct path to the positive side of the battery and the cathode must have a direct path to the negative side of the battery. the paths cannot touch or cross at any point or the circuit won't work!

the offset T-shape of the twirlycopter's rotor blades makes it spin when dropped. gravity pulls the copter down while the air creates resistance and pushes up each rotor separately, causing the copter to spin.

SUPERFUN

70

make your own!

here's a template to get you started!

cut along the solid lines. fold along the dotted lines.

try varying the size + shape of your rotor blades and the weight of your paper to see how that changes the way your copter spins!

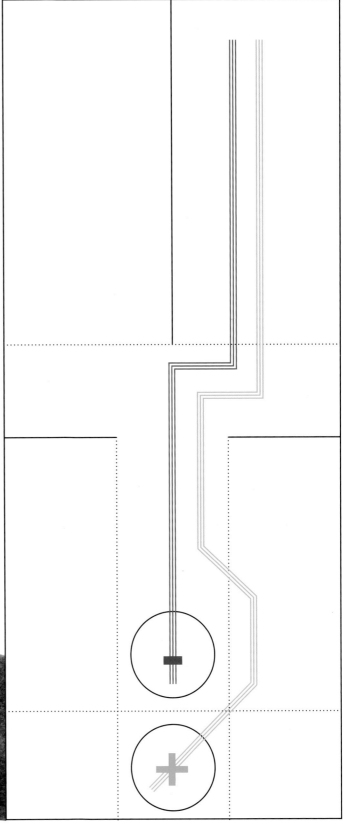

nebula jar

water-storing crystals
used in soil to hold water

water-storing beads
grow 200 times bigger!

diaper filling
super absorbent, easy to find

maker checklist

- mason jar
- small bowls + spoons
- water
- water-storing beads
- water-storing crystals
- diaper filling
- food coloring
- glitter
- liquid glycerin
- white paint
- pipette or dropper

use one or a mix

beads   crystals   diaper filling

what's a nebula?

It's a space cloud made of dust and gases that include (and sometimes produce!) stars. There are lots of nebulas in our galaxy, but one that can be seen by the naked eye is the Orion Nebula. It is 2,000 times bigger than the sun!

 First, grow your water crystals and beads! Pour your water crystals, beads, and diaper filling into individual containers and add water. They will grow and gel at different speeds. (The diaper is fastest, and the beads take longest—up to 6 hours.)

 Color your water-absorbing gels with food coloring. Go for colors that remind you of space.

 Layer your various gels with the occasional sprinkle of glitter until your jar has been filled.

 Make your cloud mixture by combining a few drops of liquid glycerin with about a tablespoon of white paint. The glycerin is optional but thins the paint to help it run.

 Using a pipette, inject your jar with streams of your mixture. This makes the cloud!

cool!

lava tubes

ever heard the expression "like oil and water"?

maker checklist

clear glass bottle

food coloring or liquid water colors

candy colorants— these mix into oils!

measuring cups or mixing bowls

stir sticks

a water base

an oil base

combo 1 *(this page)*

water base: corn syrup

oil base: baby oil

combo 2 *(that page)*

water base: water

oil base: vegetable oil

sodium bicarbonate tablet

Here you see blue and yellow combine, momentarily, into green.

tinker more!

 Pour the water base (water or corn syrup) into one measuring cup and the oil base into another. You should pour enough of each so that when combined, they will fill the bottle. Eyeball it!

 Color the water base with a few drops of food coloring.

 Color the oil base with a few drops of candy colorant. The candy colorant will mix into oil-based substances, but food coloring will not.

hint! Lightly touch your stir stick to the colorant and mix it in a bit at a time. A little goes a long way!

 Pour the water base into your tall jar, about halfway up, and then add the oil. Leave a tiny bit of space (air) at the top, and screw the cap on tightly!

 Tilt the bottle back and forth. Look for the beautiful line of color where the two liquids meet.

Drop a sodium biocarbonate tablet into the water-and-vegetable-oil combination and watch it fizz!

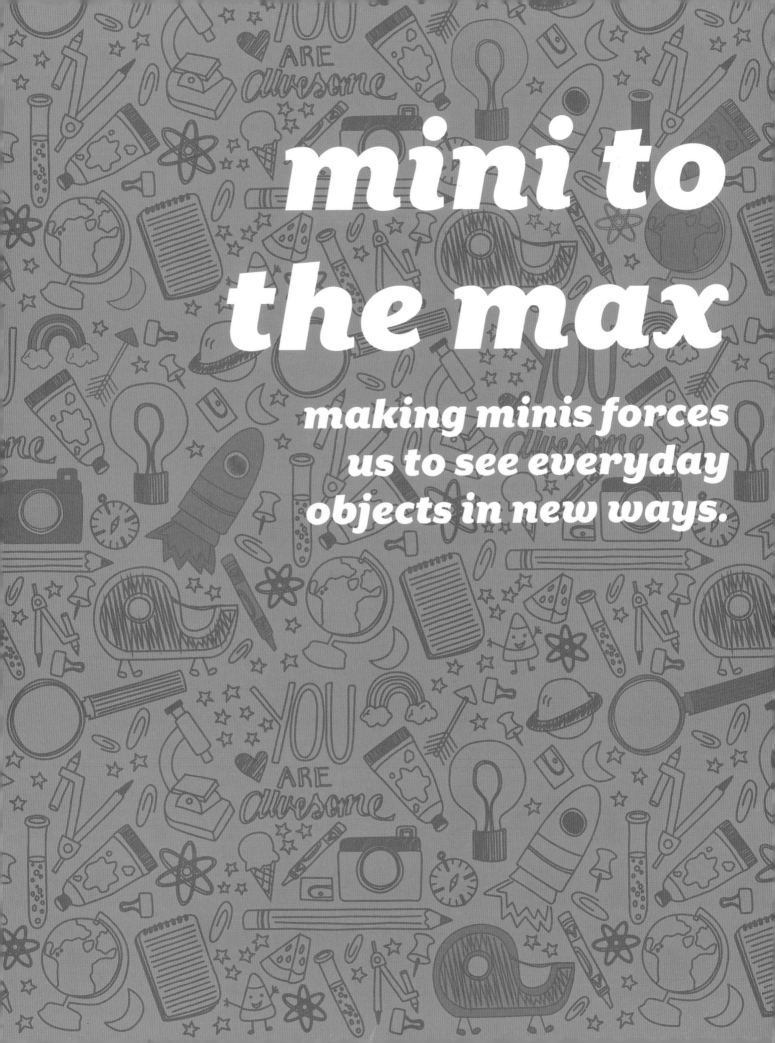

mini to the max

making minis forces us to see everyday objects in new ways.

mini terrariums

create your own little ecosystem

We love terrariums because they combine a few of our favorite things—nature, décor, and things in miniature. You don't need to know a lot about gardening or houseplants to make and keep a terrarium. And once they're done, they take only a bit of attention, time, and space.

Plus, they're super fun to make!

I have a great idea!

maker checklist

small tin or other containers

stones or gravel

different colored mosses

air plants

fun little toy creatures

SERIOUSLY Too cute

FUN FACT

What's an air plant? Air plants can grow—and thrive—without soil! Air plants are so easy to grow because they get almost all of the water and nutrients they need through their specialized leaves.

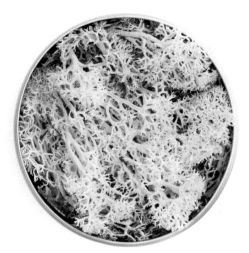

once a closed terrarium reaches a state of equilibrium—meaning it has just the right amount of moisture; not too much or too little—it will take care of itself!

. . . a few air plants . . .

. . . a little moss . . .

. . . some soil, wood chips, and pebbles . . .

we cut out an opening in our clear lid to let water and air into our terrarium.

create your own little ecosystem

 Find a small tin or jar for your terrarium. We used a tin with an opening cut in the plastic lid. You can use a small glass or even a spice jar.

 Layer small rocks, moss, and other air plants in your tin or jar. You want to use mosses and air plants because they don't require soil and don't need to be watered regularly.

 Hide a little toy creature in your miniature landscape just for fun!

Care for your terrarium by misting with water from a spray bottle every few days.

. . . and a tiny toy creature for fun

bristle bots

maker checklist

- toothbrush head
- double-sided foam tape
- 4 ball pins
- vibrating pager motor
- 3V coin battery
- masking tape

1 With an adult's help, carefully cut or snap off the head of the toothbrush from the handle. Trim any rough edges with scissors.

2 Attach the legs. Put a bit of double-sided foam tape on top of the toothbrush head and attach the pins by sticking them into the foam. You will need to bend the pins slightly to angle the legs toward the floor.

3 Attach the motor to the battery. Use a bit of masking tape to firmly connect one of the motor wires to one side of the battery.

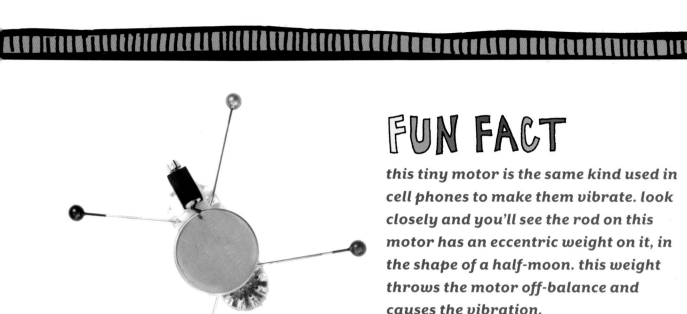

FUN FACT

this tiny motor is the same kind used in cell phones to make them vibrate. look closely and you'll see the rod on this motor has an eccentric weight on it, in the shape of a half-moon. this weight throws the motor off-balance and causes the vibration.

4 Add the battery and motor. Put another square of double-sided foam tape on top of the legs. Stick the battery to this—centered on the top of the toothbrush head—with the taped side of the battery facing down. The other bit of wire coming from the motor will be sticking up freely.

5 Turn it on! Simply tape the other motor wire to the top of the battery and watch it wiggle around!

'sup, chompers? think your big feet are a match for me?

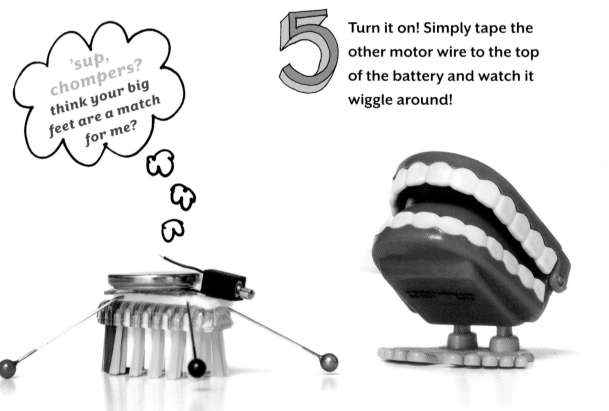

mini Mylar balloons

Mega is fun, but mini is super fun!

maker checklist

printed letters (about 2 inches high)

cotton squares (face pads)

scissors + hot glue gun

foil gift wrap

cake-pop sticks

Samantha is 6 feet tall.

the mega fun balloons are 3 feet tall.

the mini fun balloons are 3 inches tall.

YAY!

1 Make your stencils. Choose the words or letters you'd like to make and print them out in a simple, bold font about 2 inches in height. Use these as guides to make your puffy letters.

2 Make your puffy letters. Roll the cotton squares into little logs and carefully hot glue the seam to keep them from unrolling. Trim and shape to size to match your letters. Use hot glue gun to join pieces together.

you can find foil gift wrap and cake-pop sticks at most large arts & crafts stores.

3 Wrap in foil. Cut squares of foil about twice the size of the cotton letter. Lay the letter on the foil square, trace with hot glue, place a cake-pop stick on the bottom, immediately place another foil square on top as if you are making a sandwich. Press the foil down and seal against the hot glue. Then trim the excess around the edges.

emoji +
ravioli =
emojioli

look for stiffened felt sheets.
you can cut and punch them
to create clean-edged details.

difficulty: medium **emojiolis!**

maker checklist

pencil + piece of cardstock

felt sheets in yellow

scissors

stiffened felt sheets in
various colors

embroidery thread

sewing needle + pins

tacky glue

hole punch + good scissors

dry beans or rice to fill
your emojiolis

a funnel (makes it easy to fill)

1 Create a pattern by tracing a circle (3 to 4 inches in diameter) onto a piece of white cardstock. Make two circles and cut them out.

2 Pin the circles to a sheet of yellow felt and cut around the patterns so that you have two yellow felt circles.

3 Cut eyes, mouths, tongues, and all sorts of funny face details from the stiffened felt sheets.

don't they look just like emoji raviolis? emojiolis!

4 Lay out your funny face designs and glue the face parts to the circle with tacky glue. Let dry completely.

use a funnel to help fill the bean bag!

5 Stack an emoji face on top of a blank yellow circle.

6 Glue them together around the edge, leaving an opening of about ½ inch. Let dry completely.

7 Fill the felt pouch, via your ½-inch opening, with dry beans or rice. Close the opening with glue and let dry.

8 Sew the circles together around the edge, and secure with a double knot!

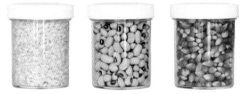

87

build-your-own
mini catapult

Use basic supplies to create a working catapult.

maker checklist

small cardboard box

3 pencils (unsharpened is best)

a few strong rubber bands

hole punch + scissors + ruler

masking tape or glue

jar lid (for the catapult bucket)

A catapult is used to send things flying. Crucial as a weapon during medieval times, this simple machine makes use of stored energy (as tension) to release the projectile, called the payload, through an arc into the air.

wheeeeee ... !

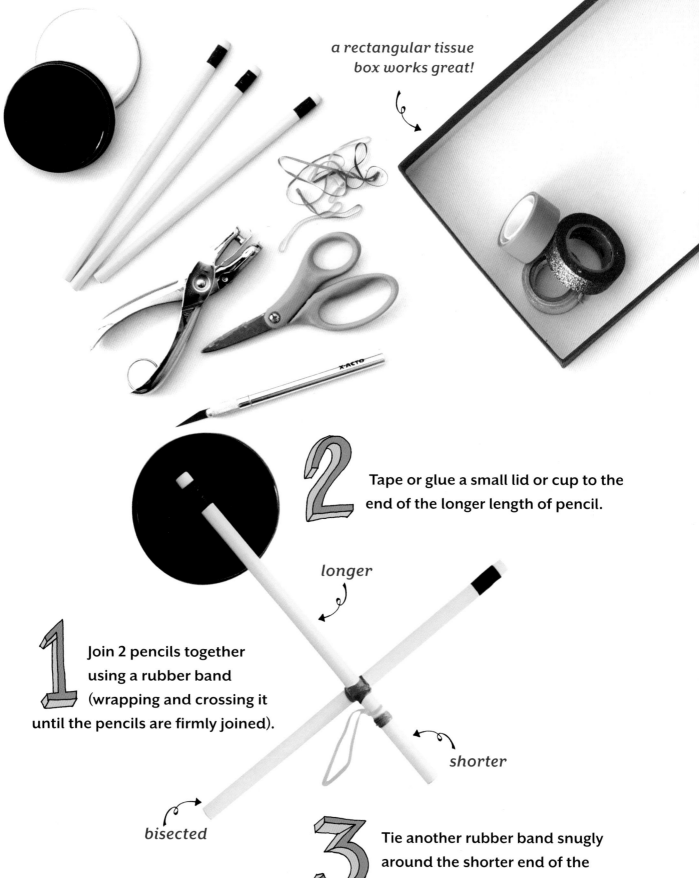

a rectangular tissue
box works great!

2 Tape or glue a small lid or cup to the
end of the longer length of pencil.

longer

1 Join 2 pencils together
using a rubber band
(wrapping and crossing it
until the pencils are firmly joined).

shorter

bisected

3 Tie another rubber band snugly
around the shorter end of the
pencil, just below the intersection.

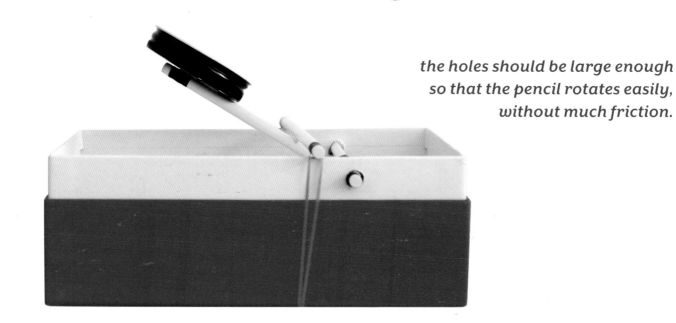

*the holes should be large enough
so that the pencil rotates easily,
without much friction.*

4 Punch a hole in the side of the box, toward the top, and about 3 inches from the end. Measure and punch a matching hole on the other side.

5 Place the third pencil across the top of the box. Secure it in place by wrapping a rubber band around one end of the pencil, down under the box, and up and around the other end. This acts as a "stopper" to keep the catapult arm from rotating too far forward and launching the payload into the ground!

*experiment with the position
of the stopper to get the
maximum angle for your
launch!*

6 Assemble the catapult arm in the box by placing one end of the pencil through one hole, and the other end of the pencil through the other hole.

7 Punch a small hole in the back of the box, toward the bottom, and feed the free rubber band through it, taping it firmly to the back of the box to keep it from slipping back inside. You can also thread a paper clip through it to hold it in place.

anatomy of a catapult

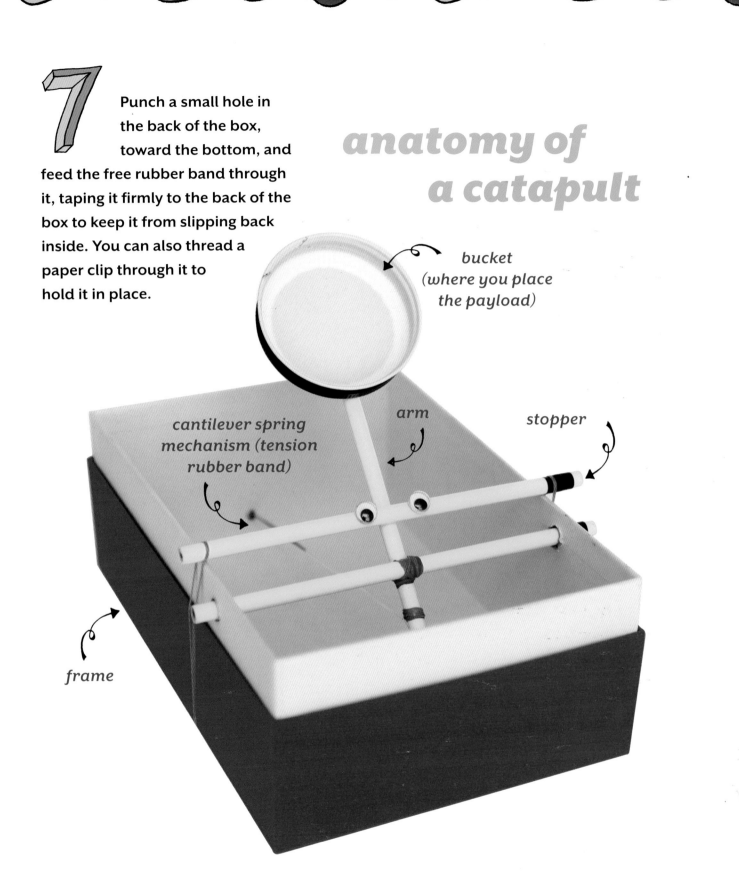

bucket
(where you place
the payload)

cantilever spring
mechanism (tension
rubber band)

arm

stopper

frame

load it . . . pull it back . . . and let 'er fly!

DIY dollhouse

SUPER FUN

big ideas for a tiny world!

There are no steps to follow—this is free-form creativity! Reimagine, recombine, and recreate your various objects, papers, and boxes into a miniature world assemblage. See our examples for different ideas, and then look for inspiration in tiny household items and other miniature objects that surround you.

MAJOR CUTENESS AHEAD

maker checklist

small boxes (wood or cardboard)

paper scraps

fabric scraps

lots of crafty bits

white glue

Really awesome

mini
clothespin people

everyday objects become a family of friends.

maker checklist

doll clothespins

embroidery thread

hot glue gun

markers (optional)

we wound red and white thread at the same time to create the stripes on this shirt.

1 First, wind your thread around the top of your doll pin to create the shirt.

2 Next, wind thread around both legs to create a skirt, or wind it in and around each leg (figure-eight style!) to create shorts or pants.

SO STINKIN' CUTE

3 Make sure to end each piece of thread with a knot around the pin.

4 To finish, make your doll's hair, and secure it to the top of the pin with a dab of hot glue.

XO

5 Add a face or shoes with markers if you'd like!

teeny tiny

big *little* cuteness

tiny things are just so cute, right?!

In Japan, there's a special name for it, and it could be that we've followed their lead and picked up on the trend here. The word in Japanese is *kawaii*, and it roughly means lovable, cute, and adorable. But it literally translates to "one's face is aglow." Kind of like when you blush. Originally, teenagers embraced the idea in fashion, handwriting, toys, personal behaviors, food, and more. Today, everyone in Japan enjoys the idea of cuteness wherever it can be found. And the idea has expanded beyond Japan as well.

small = so so cute!

HOW TO

itty-bitty colored pencils

First, use scissors to carefully cut toothpicks in half.

Next, color your pencils using markers—except for that last little bit below the point.

Then add a dot of color at the point to create the "tip" of your pencil.

Finally, store your pencils in a tiny cup, like a thimble or glue-stick cap!

Glue Stick Premium Non-Toxic

adorbs

tiny houses

Tiny houses have become more popular over the last few years. The typical tiny house is about 100 to 400 square feet. Ask your parents how that compares to your home. Would you want to live in a tiny house? (If you look up "tiny houses" on the Internet, you'll find lots of fun—and cute—images to scroll through for inspiration!)

this table is the plastic piece that comes in the middle of your delivery pizza!

tiny **hangers**

paperclips + pliers + wire cutter

Follow these for visual steps to bend your paperclips into mini hangers.

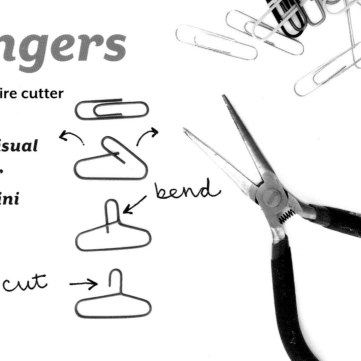

bend

cut →

tinier **markers**

polymer clay

Mold out of colorful polymer clay and bake at 275 degrees for 10–15 minutes.

SO small!

SO SO CUTE

tiniest lollipops

polymer clay + craft wire + clear tape

Cut your craft wire into small (1 cm) pieces. Use pliers to hook one end of your wire so it doesn't slip out of the polymer clay. Add a tiny ball of polymer clay and gently flatten between your fingers. Bake at 275 degrees for 10–15 minutes. Once cooled, fold a tiny piece of clear tape over the candy to make your lollipop look wrapped.

SWEET

itty bitty

upcycled furniture

trash to treasure

Go through your junk drawer and recycle bin to collect caps, lids, and other colorful and quirky odds and ends. . . . Then, with a little imagination (and a hot glue gun!) you can turn these random bits into awesome furniture and accessories for your miniature house.

All sorts of craft supplies and tiny objects can be made into miniature furniture and accessories, like:

- craft wire
- toothpicks
- plastic bottle caps
- craft foam + fabric scraps
- oven-bake clay
- markers
- pony beads
- construction paper
- whatever you have lying around!

> this pedestal sink is just a sports-bottle cap turned upside-down. the toilet is made from dental floss, a bottle cap, and a disposable contact lens package!

crazy cool

make it, wear it

you don't need a sewing machine for these projects, and for some of them you don't even need a needle and thread!

difficulty: medium

duct tape wallet

maker checklist

Tyvek envelope

your favorite colored and patterned duct tape

ruler + pencil + scissors

a snap, Velcro, or rubber band

1 Measure and cut a 3 x 7-inch rectangle of Tyvek. Cut this piece from the bottom or top of the envelope so that it includes the fold and you actually have a "pocket" that is 3 x 7 inches. This will be the main part of your wallet.

2 Tape the short side of the rectangle closed to finish the main pocket.

EP13C July 2013
OD: 11.625 x 15.125

...kee to U.S., select APO/FPO/DPO, and select international destinations. See DMM and IMM at pe.usps.com for complete details.

3 Cut additional rectangles of Tyvek to use for smaller pockets on the interior of the wallet.

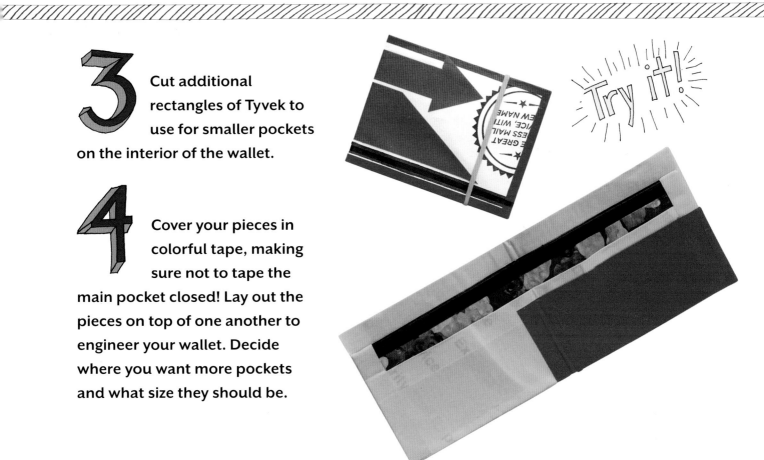

Try it!

4 Cover your pieces in colorful tape, making sure not to tape the main pocket closed! Lay out the pieces on top of one another to engineer your wallet. Decide where you want more pockets and what size they should be.

5 Once you have designed the additional parts of the wallet, tape them into place as well.

6 Fold in half, and add a snap, Velcro, or simple rubber band (our pick!) to keep the wallet closed.

7 Add your necessary wallet items, then use and enjoy!

no-sew T-shirt tote

maker checklist

T-shirt to upcycle

good scissors

pony beads (optional)

nimble fingers + a little patience!

1 Lay the T-shirt flat. Cut off the arms just past the seam and cut away the neckline in a deep U shape. Cut off the bottom hem and discard. Now you already have your main shape!

2 Cut strips up from the bottom of the tee, about 4 inches long and ½ inch wide.

3 Moving from left to right, tie the front strip to the back strip; make a double knot and pull tight. This will both help the bottom of the bag stay secure, and will give the tee a tote-like shape.

4 Now move from left to right again and tie the adjacent strips to each other. This will close any small holes in the bottom of the tote.

5 Add some beads for color and fun.

6 Wear and use!

no-sew tulle tutus

loop and tie your way to a colorful tulle tutu!

maker checklist

tulle

elastic

scissors

a safety pin

a book helps make it easier to tie on the tulle.

1 Make an elastic band to fit your waist. We used a 1-inch-wide strip of colorful elastic and pinned it securely with a safety pin. (You can also use a quick whip stitch if you like.)

2 Cut the tulle into strips. This is not an exact science! Variation in the size of the strips will make for a more creative tutu. But, as a rule of thumb, the width should be 3 to 6 inches. Length should be about twice as long as the length you want for your tutu.

3 Fit the elastic band over a book to make it easier to slip the tulle under and around.

4 Fold a strip of tulle in half and slip the folded loop under the elastic. Feed the two loose ends through the loop and pull to tighten.

5 Tie the strips of tulle onto the elastic band, working your way around the entire waistband until the tulle is full and tulle-licious!

galaxy
sneakers

maker checklist

newspaper or plastic
   tablecloth

black canvas sneakers

masking tape

textile paints

paint brushes + sponges

tiny rhinestones or sequins
   (optional)

1 Cover your work surface with newspaper or a plastic tablecloth.

SWEET

if you use glow-in-the-dark paint, your kicks will, well, glow in the dark!

 **2** Remove the shoes' laces and mask the soles with tape to keep the paint from getting on this area.

 3 Sponge or blot your paints onto your canvas sneakers in a random pattern. We stuck with blues, purples, and gold to create a galaxy effect.

 **4** Flick specks of white paint onto your sneakers to create tiny stars. We recommend glow-in-the-dark paint!

 5 Add some rhinestones or sequins for some extra sparkle! Give them a spot of hot glue to stick.

 6 Let dry, wear, and prepare for some out-of-this-world compliments!

difficulty: *medium*
pom-pom bag swag

turn little bundles of embroidery thread into colorful tassels.

craft yarn is perfect for pom-poms.

mix + match colors to create a palette.

make pom-poms and tassels, then string them together for some serious bag swag. . . .

maker checklist

scissors

fork

craft yarn

embroidery thread

string

colorful plastic beads

large eye needle

key chain clasps

yes please

fork pom-poms

1 Cut a 6-inch piece of yarn. Thread it through the middle tines of the fork, letting it hang loose

2 Now wind lots of yarn around all the tines. The more you wind, the fuller your pom-pom will be.

3 Bring the ends of the loose piece up and around the ball of yarn. Tie it with a strong knot.

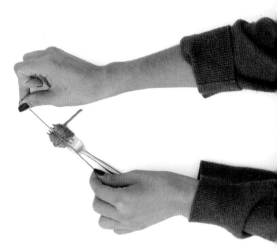

4 Slide the pom-pom off the fork. Slip one blade of the scissors through the looped ends and cut carefully. Do this on both sides. Trim the ends to make a round shape.

easy-peasy tassels

1 Tie a piece of string around the center of a skein of embroidery thread.

tie here.

fold in half.

2 Fold the skein in half so that the string you just tied is at the top.

wrap here.

3 Wind embroidery thread around the tassel, leaving a "head" on the top, and tie off.

trim the bottom.

4 Trim the bottom of the tassel so the fringed edge is even.

make your own!

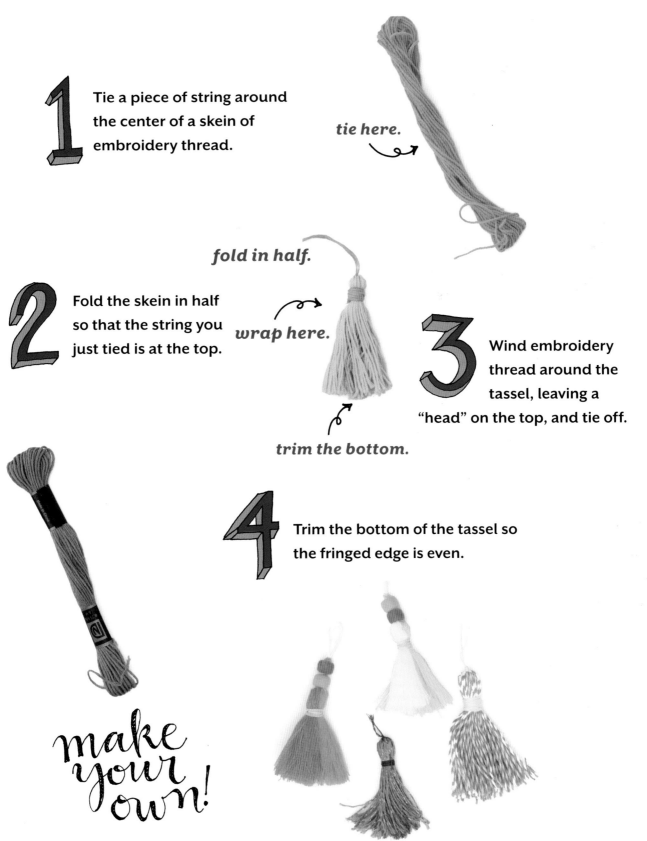

simple circle loom

use this clever finger-weaving trick on your amazing circle loom!

maker checklist

yarn

old, colorful T-shirts cut into strips

large PVC pipe fitting (6 inches) or empty takeout soup container

masking tape or duct tape

permanent markers

scissors

i love this stuff

amazing

finger weaving step-by-step

 1 Pinch the tail of the yarn between your thumb and palm. Wrap the long end behind your index finger, weaving it in and out across your hand.

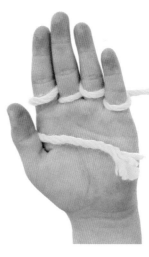 **2** Wrap the yarn back around the front of your hand, again weaving in and out so it is now looped around each finger.

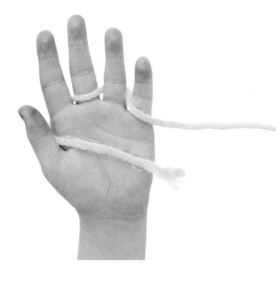

 **3** Repeat the first two steps so that you now have two rows of yarn woven through your fingers.

4 Pull the lower loop up over the top loop, and over the top of your finger. Do these at each finger. Then weave another row across your fingers and repeat!

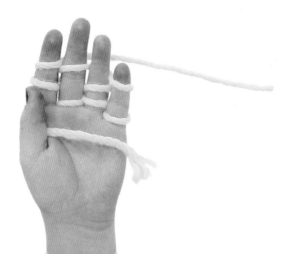

make your own yarn!

cut and stretch strips of colorful old tees and tie together to make your own yarn.

 Cut the T-shirts into strips about 1 inch wide. Stretch them out so that the edges soften and curl inward. Tie them together in a fun pattern so that you have a big fat ball of "T-shirt yarn."

 Securely tape the permanent markers in place around the outside of the pipe fitting. They should be equally distanced, with the cap portion extending above the top of the pipe fitting.

construct your loom!

 Taking up your ball of yarn, pinch a 6-inch tail against the loom and hold in place securely. Start weaving by looping the yarn inside, then outside, of each alternating marker post. Continue this pattern until you have two loops of yarn around each marker.

 Starting at the first marker, pull the bottom loop over the top loop, slipping it up and over the cap toward the center of the loom. Continue this around the loom.

to use the loom, use the same technique as finger weaving!

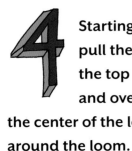 Once you get back to the start, weave another layer of yarn around the markers. Then repeat the step of pulling the bottom loop up over the top loop and off the cap, into the center of the loom.

 Repeat!

 Tie on more pieces of T-shirt as you need it. The weaving will form in a tube at the center of the loom. So cool!

Morse code bracelets

use Morse code—a series of internationally recognized dots and dashes—to make a super-cool bracelet with a hidden message

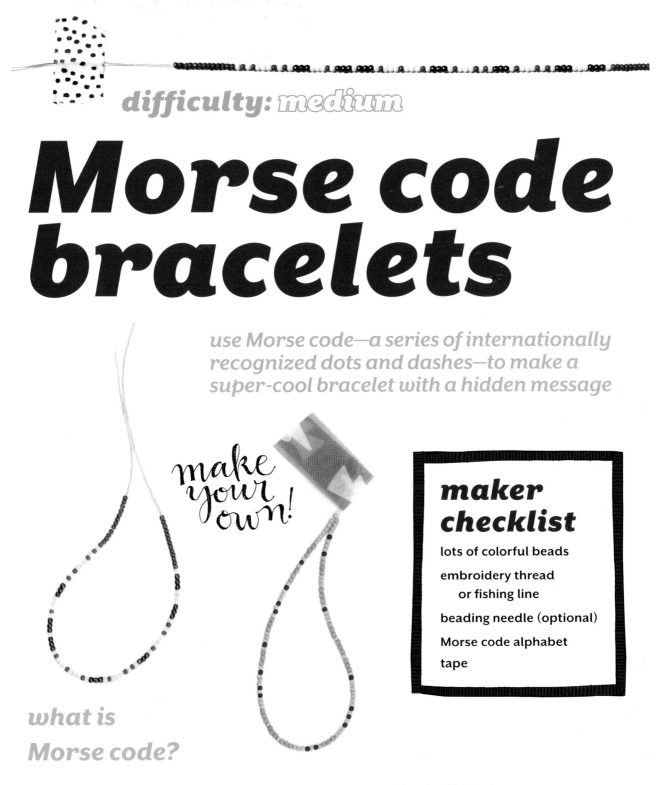

make your own!

maker checklist

lots of colorful beads

embroidery thread
   or fishing line

beading needle (optional)

Morse code alphabet

tape

what is Morse code?

Morse code is a method of communication invented in the 1830s by American artist Samuel Morse. People all around the world have used it to convey important messages throughout history!

Each symbol (dot or dash) represents a letter or number. Combined, they can communicate sentences or phrases. The most common example of Morse code is *SOS*, an internationally recognized symbol of distress, or a call for help. It's represented by three dots, three dashes, three dots.

here's an A-to-Z visual breakdown of **the international Morse code**

— • — — • • • • *this says . . .*

a dot is one unit.
a dash is three units.
the space between parts of the same letter is one unit.
the space between letters is three units (so one dash).
the space between words is seven units (so two dashes and one dot).

A • —	**N** — •	**1** • — — — —
B — • • •	**O** — — —	**2** • • — — —
C — • — •	**P** • — — •	**3** • • • — —
D — • •	**Q** — — • —	**4** • • • • —
E •	**R** • — •	**5** • • • • •
F • • — •	**S** • • •	**6** — • • • •
G — — •	**T** —	**7** — — • • •
H • • • •	**U** • • —	**8** — — — • •
I • •	**V** • • • —	**9** — — — — •
J • — — —	**W** • — —	**0** — — — — —
K — • —	**X** — • • —	
L • — • •	**Y** — • — —	
M — —	**Z** — — • •	

A·maz·ing

120

Choose your words and four colors for your bracelet:

HOW TO

one color for dots

one color for dashes

one color for spaces between letters

one color for spaces between words
(and to start and end your bracelet if you need it to be longer)

Refer to the alphabet to figure out how to bead your message. For this project, one unit = one bead.

Tape one end of the thread to a table to keep beads from sliding. String your letters, using one bead for a dot and three beads for a dash. You will also need to have a "space" between each element of the letter. (For example, if you have 3 dashes in a row, you will have a total of 9 beads. String 3 beads, then add one different color as a spacer. String another 3 beads, then a spacer, and so forth.)

Add beads in your fourth color to the start and end of your word if you need to make the bracelet longer.

can you decode our 2 bracelets?

● = dot (1 bead)
● = dash (3 beads)
○ = space between parts of letters (1 bead) and between letters (3 beads)
● = space between words (7 beads)

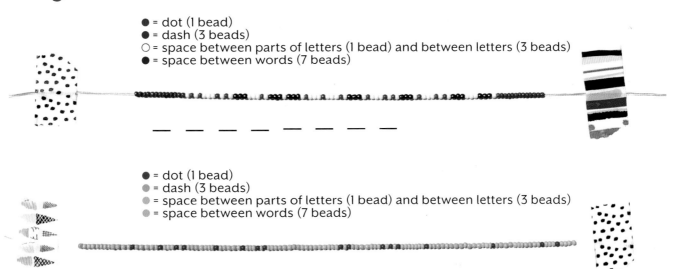

● = dot (1 bead)
● = dash (3 beads)
● = space between parts of letters (1 bead) and between letters (3 beads)
● = space between words (7 beads)

emoji pebble necklace

maker checklist

white cardstock + colored pens

glass cabochons (glass pebbles!)

scissors

round pendant trays

clear adhesive

colorful jewelry cord + clasp

adhesive that dries perfectly clear!

glass dome tile cabochon

round pendant trays

 **1** Trace the shape of the pebble onto white cardstock so you have just the right size circle.

 **2** Color a simple design, then cut out the circle.

 **3** Glue your design to the bottom of the pebble, facing up; then glue this into your pendant tray. Let dry.

 4 String onto silky jewelry cord and add a clasp or just a simple knot!

meet Curious Jane

CURIOUS JANE

Curious Jane is for girls ages 6 to 11 who like to make things! Everything we do revolves around **science** + *design* + *engineering.*

We run summer camps and workshops in and around New York City, and we publish an ad-free print magazine so that girls everywhere can have the Curious Jane experience at home.

We empower girls through making things!

about us

We're a small but passionate team, we love what we do, and we want girls to love it, too! In 2014, we were thrilled to receive a prestigious Mission Main Street Small Business Grant from Chase Bank in support of our programs for girls. That grant allowed us to grow in new ways. Each year, we offer more workshops, add new locations, and work with amazing organizations. In 2015, we launched our print magazine so that girls can try our projects at home. We are excited to grow the Curious Jane community!

meet the *Makers*

Samantha founded Curious Jane 10 years ago to give her daughters, and all girls, a place to be creative and inventive in a high-energy space. She's Southern-born, Brooklyn-based, and holds design degrees from Yale and Pratt. She loves to tinker, make, and create! Celebrating Curious Jane's 10-year anniversary, she marvels at how it has grown from *camp* to *community*, from making *things* to making a *magazine*, and from project *bin* to project *book*!

Her mini-makers, Eleanor, age 17, and Olivia, age 15, are not so "mini" anymore!

Elissa is a designer, art director, and compulsive doodler. She has her dream job at Curious Jane: doing all things creative! She dreams up ideas, makes cool things, styles photo shoots, designs the magazine, and draws lots of illustrations! You might also find her decorating a birthday cake, creating an elaborate Halloween costume, or having an epic dance party with her three kids.

Her mini-makers are Leo, age 12; Ezra, age 10; and Sylvie, age 8

Paola is a Jane of all trades—CJ's resident dabbler + food colorist + curriculum designer + workshop creator. Transforming ideas to reality, she helps research and troubleshoot projects, and she makes sure the workspace is stocked with fun tools to keep the tinkering going! In her free time, Paola loves dancing, spending time with friends in her native home of Brooklyn, and studying popular TV shows (she assures you, that is a thing).

(She has no mini-makers of her own but is dedicated to introducing her godson to the joys of making a mess!)

Caroline is a Hudson Valley–based photographer who is passionate about capturing people's stories in her images. She's photographed kids, yogis, chess grand masters, chefs, farm animals, and of course, lots of colorful CJ projects. When she's not behind the camera, you can find her working on her first feature length documentary. carolinekayephotography.com

Her mini-makers are Isadora, age 12, and Amelia, age 10.

tools/ materials/ resources

You can find these molecular gastronomy items online:

sodium alginate (seaweed extract)

calcium chloride (powdered calcium)

You can find these items at an office supply store:

transparency film (also called acetate)

brass fastener (also called a brad)

3V coin battery (CR2032)

You can find these online or at a large craft supply store (craft, sewing, baking, etc.):

white glycerin soap base (soap supply)

soap colorants (soap supply)

polyfill (sewing supply)

candy colorants (baking supply)

ball-head pins (sewing supply)

round pendant trays + cabochons (glass pebbles) to fit (craft/jewelry supply)

liquid glycerin (soap supply)

Tyvek envelope (post office)

You can find these at a grocery store or mega-store:

liquid starch

petri dishes (you can also substitute shallow plastic bowls)

classic ice-pop mold

You can find these at a hardware store:

6 feet of ¾-inch PVC pipe (or order colored PVC pipe online)

and the following PVC fittings:

1 cross

6 couplings

1 elbow

2 caps

1 male adapter

1 female adapter

PVC pipe cutter

plastic to plastic adhesive

You can find these at an electronics/ hobby supply store or online:

coin battery holder (for sewing) + conductive thread (can also find online at adafruit.com)

LED stickers (can also find online at adafruit.com)

vibrating page motor (can also find online; we like evilmadscientist.com)

copper tape (can also find online)

LED (can also find online; we like sparkfun.com and adafruit.com)

You can find these at a plant nursery:

water-storing beads

water-storing crystals (you could also check the plant section of a hardware store)

air plants (can also find these at a botanic garden or online)

moss